POGAHONTAS

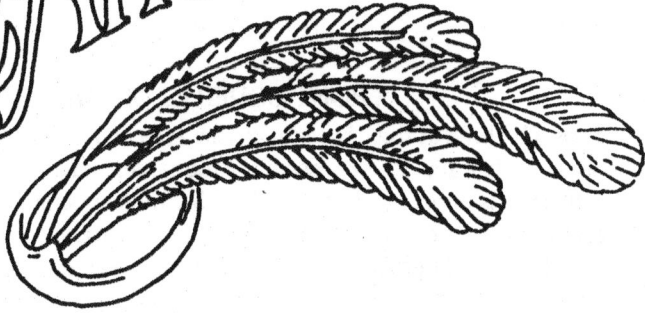

by

~Stuart E. Brown, Jr.,

CLEARFIELD

FRONT COVER ILLUSTRATION

The Indians who lived in the Chesapeake Bay area in the early 1600's and those who lived on the Carolina banks in the late 1500's were essentially the same, and a good indication as to how Pocahontas looked in about 1612 is afforded by the ca. 1584-5 Carolina banks water color done by John White. Unlike many of the artists of the Old World, White subordinated the tendency to Europeanize the Indians' facial features and in this illustration the only known error is that the lady has two right feet. Courtesy The Trustees of the British Museum.

BACK COVER ILLUSTRATION

This illustration is pure legend. Partridge's statue gives Pocahontas European facial features and clothes her improperly, but somehow the new-fallen snow conveys the idea of her great tragedy. Courtesy Colonial National Historical Park (Yorktown).

Originally published, 1989
The Pocahontas Foundation

Reprinted for
Clearfield Company, Inc., by
Genealogical Publishing Co., Inc.
Baltimore, Maryland
1995, 1998, 2006

International Standard Book Number: 0-8063-4605-1

Made in the United States of America

FOREWORD

Fact, contemporary or near-contemporary, and believed to be reasonably accurate, include all that is known about Pocahontas' appearance and her words and actions.

Suppositions, both contemporary, near-contemporary and later, are not reproduced it this volume nor are they the subject of any comment, and the same is true as regards legends.

As for illustrations of a general nature, this volume includes several pre-Pocahontas items, one or perhaps two contemporary works, and several near-contemporary engravings, most of which are believed to be reasonably accurate.

As for an illustration of Pocahontas' saving Captain John Smith, hundreds of efforts have been attempted but none can compare with the 1624 engraving reproduced in this volume.

As for an illustration of the baptism of Pocahontas, there is John G. Chapman's large (14 feet by 20 feet) late 1800's painting which hangs in the Rotunda of the United States Capitol and there is the frequently-duplicated late 1800's marriage painting done by Henry Brueckner. However, these works over-emphasize the two ceremonies and are not reproduced in this volume.

But one illustration of Pocahontas' marriage, a vignette taken from a ca. 1739 French map, is reproduced in this volume, and although it contains several inaccuracies, its title gives the Frenchmen's idea of the English colonial position in the New World.

The best known portrait of Pocahontas, i.e., the Top Hat illustration reproduced in this volume, may be the subject of some artistic license, the probabilities seeming to be that Pocahontas, appearing in London as an Indian princess, would have clothed herself in some sort of an Indian regalia and not in a court-style costume. A much better portrait, reproduced in this volume, shows her in a feathered cloak which would be quite appropriate for an Indian princess and which would be convenient if not necessary in England during the winter of 1616-17.

As for compiling this volume, the task was made much easier by kind help received from the following persons and institutions: The Adirondeck Museum, American Bank Note Company, American Philatelic Society (Frank L. Sente), The Archives of 76, The Association for the Preservation of Virginia Antiquities, Bibliotheek Der Rijksuniversiteit Te Leiden, Boston Public Library (Gail Fithian), The British

Library, The British Museum, Brown Brothers, Cassell Ltd., Chicago Historical Society, Colonial National Historical Park (Yorktown), The Colonial Williamsburg Foundation (L. Eileen Parris), The Dietz Press, Mrs. Ralph Dorsey, Gallery Mayo, Inc., Handley Library, Jamestown Festival Park, Jamestown - Yorktown Foundation (Daniel M. Hawks), Ludwell Johnson III, Kennedy Galleries, Sidney E. King, The Library of Congress (Bernard Reilly), The Magazine Antiques, The Mariners' Museum, Alister Mathews, Barbara J. Mitnick, John A. Muscalus, Museum of the American Indian, National Museum of American Art (Smithsonian Institution), National Portrait Gallery (Smithsonian Institution), The New-York Historical Society, The New York Public Library (Cheryl Raymond), James S. Patton, The Free Library of Philadelphia (Robert F. Looney), Lauren Rogers Museum of Art, Peggy and Harold Samuels, Paul W. Schmidtchen, Joyce Lee Smith, United States Banknote Coprporation, United States Capitol Historical Society, University of Virginia, The Valentine Museum, Virginia Historical Society (Virginius C. Hall, Jr., and Linda Leazer), Virginia Museum of Fine Arts, Virginia State Library (Jane H. Sumpter), College of William and Mary (Louise Lambert Kale), Woolaroc Museum, and Wunderlich & Company, Inc.

POCAHONTAS

She was of "a Coulour browne, or rather tawnye," and her age was somewhere between twelve and fourteen. She probably was roundfaced, with the fore part of her "grosse" and "thick" black hair "shaven close," and the very long "thicker part" being "tied in a pleate hanging down" to her hips. Her hands almost certainly were "pretty." Her "handsome lymbes," breast, "slender armes" and face may well have been cunningly tatooed. And she probably wore a headband or crownlet and copper-decorated beads and earrings, her head and shoulders being covered with red colored powder "mixed with the oyle of the walnut, or Beares grease." In winter this paint "armes . . . (in some measure) against the Cold" and "in Summer doth check the heat" while helping to defend "from the stinging of Muskeetoes . . . which heere breed aboundantly, amongst the marish whorts, and fenburies."[1]

Her name was Matoaka, but they called her Pocahontas, the appellation possibly being derived from the Algonkian adjective meaning "playful, sportive, frolicsome, mischievous, frisky."[2]

She was a member of one of a confederacy of some thirty well-organized, thriving agricultural and fishing tribes, who lived in approximately 160 villages widely scattered over much of the lower section of the Chesapeake Bay, and had a total population in the neighborhood 9,000.[3] And she was one of the many children of Powhatan, the confederacy's overlord or supreme werowance.[4]

Powhatan's headquarters was at the village of Werowocomoco (located on the north shore of the Pamunkey River, now the York River, some eleven miles downstream from the present city of West Point) and from there, in the spring of 1607, Powhatan learned of three white sailing ships entering the Bay.

Men from these vessels then landed on several of the southern beaches, seeing "faire meaddowes and goodly tall trees; with such fresh-waters running through the woods."[5] On one shore, there was a brief, unfriendly encounter with a few of the local tribesmen. Finally, on May 20, some forty miles up the Powhatan River, now the James River, far enough inland to promise protection from hostile Old World vessels, Captain Christopher Newport's flotilla moored to the trees.

There, on a swampy-terrained, miasmic isthmus, some of the 145 English landers quickly began to erect helter-skelter buildings. They called this new settlement Jamestown. And unknown to them, it was on a part of the hunting grounds of the Paspaheghs, one of Powhatan's overlorded tribes.

In the spring of 1607, the SUSAN CONSTANT, THE GOD-SPEED and the DISCOVERY enter the Chesapeake Bay. Illustration by E. B. Comstock from POCAHONTAS, A PRINCESS OF THE WOODS by Edward S. Ellis.

Like the other tribes of Powhatan's confederacy, the Paspaheghs opposed for territorial reasons the making of any sort of a settlement. And they also feared if they did not hate the different-dressing, different-looking people who came in large wooden ships and possessed an unusual assortment of metal tools, heavy armor, guns and cannons.

Powhatan's people knew of the Spanish Jesuit (1570-1571) murdered Pamunkey River mission.[6] They had at least heard of the ill-fated (1580's) settlement made by the English on the Carolina banks. And "the year before" or "some twoe or three yeeres before us" (prior to December of 1607), many of Powhatan's people had watched a ship enter the Pamunkey River where it was "kindly entertained by Powhatan."

This vessel later visited the Rappahannock River, being "received with like kindnesse," but the ship's captain then "slue the King" of Powhatan's Rappahannocks"and tooke of his people."[7] In addition, in September of 1603, two or more Indians, possibly others of Powhatan's people, were taken hostage.[8]

Powhatan himself had seen "people with short Coates, and Sleeves to the Elbowes, that passed . . . in Shippes." He knew of "clothed" people who lived at Ocanahonan, a Mangoak (non-Powhatan) village located near the present Virginia-North Carolina boundary, and in "the Southerly Countries also."[9] Some of these people may have been Carolina banks settlers who had gone to live with the Chesapeake Indians (in an area which lay to the south of the present Virginia city of Portsmouth), and who may well have been massacred by or on his orders. And there may have been some racial mixing: in May of 1607, Jamestown settlers saw but did not contact "a Savage Boy about the age of ten yeeres" with "a head of haire of a perfect yellow, and a reasonable white skinne."[10]

The colonists had very little understanding of their "savage" and "barbarous" counterparts, but one of the instructions given by the London Company was that "you must have great care not to offend the naturals" and you must trade before "they perceive you mean to" settle among them.[11] However, Powhatan's Indians possessed little if any gold or silver, and as late as the month of May, there was little food stored up from the previous harvest season.

As a result, there were disagreements. In a May of 1607 foray, some 200 of Powhatan's people attacked Jamestown, killing one boy and wounding seventeen men. And by June 15, the colonists had built and finished a fort.

That month, on the 22, Newport and two of the colonists' three ships set sail for England. Three days later, as a bit of relief, an Indian came with a "word of peace" from "the great Poughwaton." And on or about the July 3, an Indian delivered to President Edward Maria Wingfield a deer sent by "the Great Powhatan."[12]

Powhatan all the while kept aloof, probably fearing that the colonists would either abduct him or slay him. However, there were some noncombative contacts, and one early visitor to Jamestown may have been Pocahontas.

William Strachey, who did not arrive in the colony until 1610, described her as "a well featured but wanton young girle Powhatans daughter, . . . of the age then of 11. or 12. yeares."

And his report was that Pocahontas "sometymes resorting to our Fort . . . [would] gett the boyes forth with her into the [Jamestown's] markett place and make them wheele, falling on their hands turning their heeles upwardes, whome she would follow, and wheele so her self naked as she was all the Fort over."[13]

As for Jamestown's "boyes," five came out on the first voyage.

And as for "naked," Strachey wrote:

> the younger Indian women goe not shadowed . . . until they be nigh eleaven or twelve returnes of the Leafe old . . . but being past once 12. yeres they put on a kynd of semicinctum leathren apron (as doe our artificers or handicrafts men) before their bellies . . . .
>
> The better sort of women cover them(selves) (for the most parte) all over with skyn mantells, fynely drest, shagged and frindged at the skirt, carved and coulored, with some pretty work . . . of beasts, fowle, tortoyses, or other such Imagery. . . . some use mantells, made both of turkey feathers and other fowle so prettely wrought and woven with threeds that nothing could be discerned but the feathers, which were exceeding warm and very handsome . . . . . . sometymes in cold weather, or when they goe a hunting, or seeking the fruicts of the woodes, or gathering bents for their matts, both men and women, (to defind them from the bushes) put on a kynd of leather breeches and stockings.[14]

But even a shadowed, mantelled lady of Powhatan's confederacy, while doing cartwheels, must have appeared virtually naked.

As for the settlers, they had been told not to let the Indians "see or know of your sick" and "do not advertize the killing of any of your men." But of the 100 men and four boys left in Jamestown when the two ships set sail on June 22, only forty were alive by December, the remainder, using the James River for their drinking water as well as for their sewer, were "destroyed with cruell diseases, as Swellings [salt water poisoning], Flixes [dysentery], Burning Fevers [typhoid], and by warres."[15]

Some also "departed suddenly" but most of them "died of meere famine."[16]

Trading with the "naturals" for food stuffs thus became essential, and in December of 1607, nine men sailed up the Chickahominy River under the command of the colony's most accomplished barterer, a twenty-seven year old commoner, an ex-captain of horse who fought for the Holy Roman Empire against the Turks, and the bearer of the somewhat prototypically common name of John Smith.

4

This group, wanting to make an initial contact with Powhatan, also hoped to replenish larders and, incidentally, to find a new way to the Orient. But for easy passage the waters in the upper reaches of the Chickahominy soon proved to be too shallow. As some of the ship's men went ashore, Smith and one Indian guide pushed on ahead. And then, by chance, Smith and his guide were confronted by a large party of Powhatan's deer hunters.

In the resulting melee, Smith fatally shot two of the hunters, and while Smith and his guide were "retiring in the midst of a low quagmire," they "stept fast, into the quagmire," and Smith was "tooke . . . prisoner".

The leader of the deer hunters (and Powhatan's brother Opechancanough) then saw to it that Smith was shepherded through various sections of Powhatan's confederacy. On one occasion, stopping among the Rappahannocks, the captors decided that the short Smith could not have been the tall ship's captain who some years before had slain the tribe's werowance. At other places, Powhatan's Indians made "many strange triumphes and conjurations," and finally, in January of 1608, Smith was brought to Werowocomoco.

There two hundred "grim Courtiers stood wondering" as though Smith was "a monster," and as Smith was placed before Powhatan, "all the people gave a great shout."[17]

Powhatan there sat "before a fire upon a seat like a bedstead . . . covered with a great robe, made of Rarowcum (racoon) skinnes, and all the tayles hanging by." On either hand was "a young wench of 16 or 18 years," and on each side of the house there were "two rowes of men, and behind them as many women, with all their heads and shoulders painted red" and with "many of their heads bedecked with the white downe of Birds . . . a great chayne of white beads (hung) about their necks."[18]

Powhatan, according to Smith, was "a tall well proportioned man, with a sower looke, his head somewhat gray, his beard so thinne that it seemeth none at al, his age neare 60; of a very able and hardy body to endure any labour."[19] And in Smith's eyes, he had "such a grave and Majesticall countenance, as drave me into admiration to see such state in a naked Salvage."[20]

Opossunoquonuske, the "Queene of Appamatuck" and sister of the werowance of the Appamatucks, then approached Smith whom she had met, along with Gabriel Archer and other colonists, in May of 1607, in the country of the Appamatuck.

At that time, she came:

in selfe same fashion of state as Powatah . . . yea rather with more maiesty: she had an usher before her who brought her to the matt prepared under a faire mulberry tree, where she satt her Downe by her selfe with a stayed Countenance, she would permitt none to stand or sitt neere her: she is a fatt

5

lustie manly woman: she had much Copper about her neck, a Crownet of Copper upon her hed: she had long black haire, which hanged loose downe her back to her myddle, which only part was covered with a Deares skyn, and ells all naked. She had her woemen attending on her adorned much like her selfe (save they wanted ye Copper).[21]

At Werowocomoco, Opossunoquonuske, carrying out Powhatan's premeal practice, brought Smith "water to wash his hands" while another Indian woman "brought him a bunch of feathers, instead of a Towell to dry them."

Powhatan then "feasted" Smith, and at the end of the meal and a long consultation between Powhatan and his advisors, "two great stones were brought before Powhatan."

Smith's head was placed on one of the stones. Indians were "ready with their clubs, to beate out his braines." And when "no intreaty could prevaile," Pocahontas, Powhatan's "dearest daughter," got Smith's "head in her armes, and laid her owne upon his to save him from death."[22]

POWHATAN
Held this state & fashion when Capt. Smith
was delivered to him prisoner
1607

Within the illustration:

King Powhatan comands C: Smith to be slayne, his daughter Pokahontas beggs his life his thankfullness and how he subiected 39 of their kings. reade § history.

Pocahontas Saves Smith
This illustration taken from Smith's 1624 book probably was approved by Smith. The large-sized person in the right foreground probably is a priest.

The saving of Smith by Pocahontas may have been spontaneous or it may have been a portion of an adoption ritual or it may have been a ceremonial step preliminary to a marriage. But whatever the reason, Powhatan appeared "contented".

Smith "should live to make him hatchets," and make Pocahontas "bells, beads and, copper; for they thought him [Smith] as well of all occupations as themselves. For the King himselfe will make his owne robes, shooes, bowes, arrowes, pots; plant, hunt or do any thing so well as the rest."

Some two days after the saving of Smith by Pocahontas, Smith was taken to "a great house in the woods," and Powhatan, accompanied by "some two hundred more" of his Indians, and "more like a devill than a man," told Smith that now they were friends and that Smith should go to Jamestown and send Powhatan "two great gunnes, and a gryndstone, for which he would give him the Country of Capahowosick, and for ever esteeme him as his sonne Nantaquoud."[23]

Pocahontas then "so previaled with her father" that Smith was "safely conducted to James towne."

Smith later wrote:

> I received from this great Salvage exceeding great courtesie, especially from his sonne Nantaquaus, the most manliest, comeliest, boldest spirit, I ever saw in a Salvage, and his sister Pocahontas, the Kings most deare and wel-beloved daughter, being but a childe of twelve or thirteene years of age.[24]

In Jamestown, Smith found "about eight and thirtie miserable poore and sicke creatures, to keepe possession of all those large territories of Virginia."[25] But he also found another problem.

On the Chickahominy trip, three of Smith's command had been killed by Indians, one, George Cassen, "being stripped naked and bound to two stakes, with his backe against a great fire; then they did rippe him and burne his bowels, and dried his flesh to the bones."[26] But to give the devil his due, the colonists probably were even more cruel.

For the loss of his three men, Smith was tried in Jamestown, and probably would have been hanged had it not been for the recent arrival from England of a convoy headed by Newport.[27]

He Princes of Virginia are attyred in fuche manner as is expreffed in this figure. They weare the haire of their heades long and bynde opp the ende of thefame in a knot vnder thier eares. Yet they cutt the topp of their heades from the forehead to the nape of the necke in manner of a cokfcombe, ftirkinge a faier lóge pecher of fome berd att the Begininge of the crefte vppun their foreheads, and another fhort one on bothe feides about their eares. They hange at their eares ether thicke pearles, or fomwhat els, as the clawe of fome great birde, as cometh in to their fanfye. Moreouer They ether pownes, or paynt their forehead, cheeks, chynne, bodye, armes, and leggs, yet in another forte then the inhabitantz of Florida. They weare a chaine about their necks of pearles or beades of copper, wich they muche efteeme, and ther of wear they alfo brafelets ohn their armes. Vnder their brefts about their bellyes appeir certayne fpotts, whear they vfe to lett them felues bloode, when they are ficke. They hange before thē the fkinne of fome beafte verye feinelye dreffet in fuche forte, that the rayle hangeth downe behynde. They carye a quiuer made of fmall ruſhes holding their bowe readie bent in on hand, and an arrowe in the other, radie to defend themfelues. In this manner they goe to warr, or tho their folemne feafts and banquetts. They take muche pleafure in huntinge of deer wher of theris great ftore in the contrye, for yt is fruitfull, pleafant, and full of Goodly woods. Yt hathe alfo ftore of riuers full of diuers forts of fifhe. When they go to battel they paynt their bodyes in the moft terible manner that thei can deuife.

This illustration, a John White Carolina banks drawing as redone by Theodor de Bry, probably is a good indication of how Powhatan looked. From Harriot, Thomas. A BRIEF AND TRUE REPORT OF THE NEW FOUND LAND OF VIRGINIA (1590).

This infusion of personnel and supplies coupled with the "plenties" Smith had seen and "the state and bountie of Powhatan" revived the colonists' "dead spirits (especially the love of Pocahontas) as all mens feare was abandoned." And "the Salvages . . . every other day repaired, with such provisions that sufficiently did save them from hand to mouth: part always they brought him as presents from their Kings, or Pocahontas" . . .

. . . "such was the weaknesse of this poore Common-wealth, as had the Salvages not fed us, we directly had starved.[28]

"And this reliefe . . . was commonly brought us by this Lady Pocahontas."[29]

Powhatan, meanwhile, expressed a desire to see Newport whom Powhatan's Indians "esteemed . . . as an Oracle"[30] and in February of 1608, Newport, Smith, and about thirty or forty men sailed to Werowocomoco.

There Powhatan sat "upon his bed of mats, his pillow of leather imbrodered (after their rude manner with pearle and white Beads) his attyre a faire robe of skinnes as large as an Irish mantell . . . on each side his house sat twentie of his Concubines . . . Before those sat his chiefest men in like order in his arbour-like house . . . Foure or five hundred people made a guard . . . ."

There were "feasts" as well as "feates, dauncing and singing, and such like mirth," and that night Smith and his nine men "quartered" with Powhatan.

The next morning, Newport came ashore, engaged in a peace talk, and gave Powhatan a hostage, thirteen year old Thomas Savage, while receiving as a counter-hostage Namontack, Powhatan's "trustie servant, and one of a shrewd, subtill capacities."[31]

Namontack, on April 10, sailed for England with Newport.

Later in April, as a result of a trade disagreement, Smith captured seven Paspaheghans, and Powhatan, hearing of this capture, "sent his Daughter" who, according to Smith.

> not only for feature, countenance, and proportion, much exceedeth any of the rest of his [Powhatan's] people, but for wit, and spirit, [she is] the only Nonpariel of his Country.

Pocahontas was accompanied by Powhatan's "most trustie messenger, called Rawhunt, as much exceeding in deformitie of person, but of subtill wit and crafty understanding." Rawhunt "with a long circumstance" told Smith "how well Powhatan loved and respected mee, and in that I should not doubt any way of his kindnesse, he had sent his child, which he most esteemed, to see me." Rawhunt also recounted how Powhatan to "his little Daughter had taught this lesson also: not taking notice at all of the Indeans that had beene prisoners three daies, till that morning that she saw their fathers and friends come quietly, and in good tearmes to entreate their libertie."[32]

Pocahontas took "presents to execuse him [Smith] of the injuries done by some rash untoward Captaines." And after Smith gave the prisoners "what correction he saw fit [and] used them well a day or two after," he "delivered them to Pocahontas, for whose sake onley he fayned to have saved their lives."[33]

This delivery was done at or near "the Church, and after prayer." And Pocahontas was "requited, with such trifles as contented her."[34]

In June of 1608, Smith, in order to explore the Bay, sailed out from Jamestown and did not return until September.

In the interim, Newport came back from England, bringing with him more personnel (two women and seventy-eight other settlers), the hostage Namontack, and instructions from the Virginia Company that Powhatan was to be crowned Emperor.

Smith and four other colonists were then sent to Werowocomoco to "intreat" Powhatan to come to Jamestown but Powhatan was some thirty miles away, and while awaiting his return, "Pocahontas and her women entertained Captaine Smith in this manner":

In a fayre plaine field they made a fire . . . and suddainly amongst the woods was heard such a hydeous noise and shreeking, that the English betooke themselves to their armes, and seized on two or three old men . . . supposing Powhatan with all his power was come to surprise them. But presently Pocahontas came, willing [the colonists] to kill her if any hurt were intended, and the beholders, which were men, women, and children, satisfied the Captaine there was no such matter.

Then presently . . . thirtie young women came naked out of the woods, onely covered behind and before with a few greene leaves, their bodies all painted, some of one colour, some of another, but all differing . . their leader had a fayre payre of Bucks hornes on her head, and an Otters skinne at her girdle, and another at her arme, a quiver of arrowes at her backe, a bow and arrowes in her hand; the next had in her hand a sword, another a club, another a pot-sticke; all horned alike: the rest every one with their severall devises.

These fiends with most hellish shouts and cryes, rushing from among the trees, cast themselves in a ring about the fire, singing and dauncing with most excellent ill varietie, oft falling into their infernall passions, and solemnly againe to sing and daunce.

And after "having spent neare an houre in this Mascarado . . . they departed."

Then the Indian women "reaccommodated themselves" and "solemnly invited [Smith] to their lodgings, where he was no sooner within the house, but all these Nymphes more tormented him then ever, with crowding, pressing, and hanging about him, most tediously crying, Love you not me? love you not me?

"This salvation ended, the feast was set, consisting of all the Salvage dainties they could devicse: some attending, others singing and dauncing about them." Finally, when the "mirth . . . ended," the Indians "with fire-brands in stead of Torches" conducted him to his lodging.[35]

The next day came Powhatan.

As for the planned coronation, it was held not at Jamestown but at Werowocomoco. Powhatan refused to be a vassal. And for all intents and purposes, the ceremony was farcical.[36]

In September of 1608, Smith was elected president of Jamestown's council, and all the while, Pocahontas "with her wilde traine freely frequented" Jamestown as much as she did "her fathers habitation."

But troubles between Powhatan and the colonists slowly worsened, and Smith wrote:

> . . . when inconstant Fortune turned our peace to warre, this tender Virgin [Pocahontas] would still not spare to dare to visit us, and by her our jarres have beene oft appeased, and our wants still supplyed; were it the policie of her father thus to employ her, or the ordinance of God thus to make her his instrument, or her extraordinarie affection to our Nation, I know not.

On January 12, 1609, Smith, hoping to reawaken friendship with Powhatan and to promote new trade, visited Werowocomoco. Although the exchange was guarded and the trade though made was far from agreeable, some of Powhatan's Indians "with all the merry sports they could devise, spent the time till night" entertaining Smith and his men at Smith's camp.

Then, the entertainers returned to Powhatan.

But "in that darke night" Powhatan's "dearest jewell and daughter, came through the irksome woods, and told our Captaine great cheare should be sent us by and by: but Powhatan and all the power he could make, would after come [and] kill" Smith and party while "at supper."

Pocahontas also warned that if Smith and his friends "would live, she wished us presently to bee gone."

Prior to departing, the grateful Smith offered Pocahontas "such things as shee delighted in . . . but with the teares running down her cheekes, she said shee durst not be seene to have any: for if Powhatan should know it, she were but dead, and so shee ranne away by her selfe as she came."[37]

12

Several days later, Master Richard Wiffin, arriving by canoe, lodged one night with Powhatan. But not finding Smith at Werowocomoco, and "perceiving such preparation for warre," Wiffin assured himself "some mischiefe was intended." Pocahontas then "hid him for a timee," sent her father's Indians who pursued him "the cleane contrary way," and permitted Wiffin to escape.[38]

Meanwhile, Powhatan wanted to be a greater distance from the colonists, and towards the end of January of 1609, he moved his residence to near Orapaks which was located on the upper reaches of the Chickahominy River, some fifty miles away from Jamestown.

Smith during this period began to expand the enterprise, moving some of the colonists to areas other than Jamestown. His determination also saved many lives: of the 200 left when Newport sailed for England in November of 1608, "there died but seven," plus the eleven lost in a boating accident. And in mid-August, the colony's personnel was greatly increased when six storm-tossed ships brought in 300 newcomers.

But in September 1609, as Smith was returning from a trip to the falls of the James River (near what is now the city of Richmond) and was sleeping in his boat, "accidentallie, one fired his powder-bag."

The explosion "tore the flesh from his body and thighes, nine or ten inches square in a most pittifull manner" and "to quench the tormenting fire", Smith "leaped overboard into the deepe river."

Unfortunately, there was neither a "Chirurgian" or "Chirurgery" in the boat or at Jamestown where Smith was the subject of much controversy—George Percy called Smith "an Ambityous unworthy and vayneglorious fellowe Attempteinge to take all Mens Authoreties from them"—and the severely wounded Smith resigned as president and went back to England for treatment.[39]

At about the time of Smith's accident, Pocahontas helped Henry Spelman (about the same age as Pocahontas) escape being a hostage with Powhatan, and to serve instead as a hostage to the more genial Patawomeke tribe who dwelt on the Potomac River.[40]

As for Smith, the colonists "alwaies" told the Indians that Smith was dead and "after a long and troublesome warre . . . betwixt" Powhatan and the colony, Pocahontas "was not heard of," the only exception being Strachey's writing that in about 1610, Pocahontas was "marryed to a pryvate Captayne called Kocoum."[41]

THE
GENERALL HISTORIE
OF
Virginia, New-England, and the Summer
Iſles: with the names of the Adventurers,
Planters, and Governours from their
firſt beginning An: 1584. to this
preſent 1624.

Meanwhile, for the colony, the "starving time" winter of 1609-1610 was horrible; the settlers "fedd uponn horses and other beastes as long as they Lasted" and "weare gladd to make shifte with vermine as doggs Catts Ratts and myce," with "fishe thatt came to Nett" and with "Bootes shoes or any other leather." And when those were "Spente and devoured," some colonists were "inforced to searche the woodes and to feede upon Serpents and snakes and to digge the earth for wylde and unknowne Rootes where many of our men weare Cutt off of and slayne by the Salvages." Some colonists also "Licked upp the Bloode which hathe fallen from their weake fellowes" and one "murdered his wyfe Ripped the childe out of her woambe and threw itt into the River and after chopped the Mother in pieces and salted her for his foode."[42]

Of the 500 settlers on hand at the time Smith left Virginia, there remained within six months "not past sixtie men, women and children, most miserable and poor creatures."[43] But by the winter of 1611-12, and despite adversities, the colony was recovering and expanding.

In March 1612, Pocahontas, "residing some three months or longer" among the Patawomekes, being "imploied thither, as a shop-keepers to a Fare, to exchange some of her fathers commodities for theirs," learned that a ship from Jamestown commanded by Samuel Argall had anchored near the village of Pastancy.[44]

The Abduction of Pocahontas

In the upper center, the second ship is a mystery as is the more distant portion in which two ships and a small boat are moored, and soldiers are burning an Indian town—this burning probably took place on the Pamunkey River in March of 1614.

This illustration is one of four pictures done by George Keller for *EIN WARHAFETIGER UND GRUNDTLICHER BERIGHT VON DEM JTZIGEN ZUSTANDT DER LANDT-SCHAFFT VIRGINIEN,* a 1617 Dutch translation of *HAMOF*

HAMOR was also reprinted in German in 1618 as a part of Theodore De Bry's *GREAT VOYAGES*. It was similarly reprinted in Latin in 1619. And the four illustrations used in the German and Latin imprints, differ slightly from those used in the 1617 translation. *Courtesy Virginia State Library.*

"Desirous to renue hir familiaritie with the English, and delighting to see them", Pocahontas went to the waterside along with Argall, Japazaws (the Pastancy werowance), and Japazaws' wife, the latter of whom expressed "a great and longing desire to goe aboorde, and see the shippe, which being there three or foure times before, she had never seene."

Japazaws, however, appeared angry, deeming his wife's request "unnecessary." But his wife wept, Japazaws "gave her leave to goe aboard," and Pocahontas, as a result of Japazaws' wife's "earnest perswasions," also went aboard and "to supper."

After dining, Japazaws and his wife has "some conference with" Argall and then "to sleep they went." But Pocahontas, "lodged in the Gunners roome", and "being most possessed with feare, and desire of returne, was first up, and hastened Japazaws to be gon".

Japazaws and his wife were permitted to go back ashore, but Argall stated that he would "reserve" Pocahontas in order to ransom the eight English men, plus "many swords, peeces, and other tooles" that her father, Powhatan, had captured and kept.

Of course, Argall, Japazaws, and Japazaws' wife acted fraudulently.

Argall, having learned that Pocahonotas was with the Patawomekes, resolved to "procure hir captive," and going ashore, was met by Japazaws and by Ensign Swift whom Argall, the voyage before, had left as a hostage.

Argall told Japazaws that if he did not betray Pocahontas, he and Japazaws "would be no longer (adopted) brothers nor friends." Japazaws "alleaged that if hee undertake the business, then Powhatan would make warres upon him and his people." However, Argall promised to join Japazaws if it became necessary to fight Powhatan, and to use Pocahontas "withall faire, and gentle entreaty." Thereupon, Japazaws conferred with his brother, the werowance of the Patawomekes, and following a council meeting, the Patawomekes expressed approval.

In the scheme, Japazaws used his wife as "an instrument (which sex have ever bin most powerfull in beguiling inticements)." And as a reward, Japazaws received "a small Copper kettle, and som other les valuable toies so highly by him esteemed, that doubtlesse he would have betraied his own father for them."

Pocahontas, kidnapped, "began to be exceeding pensive, and discontented." Thereafter "much a doe there was to perswade her [Pocahontas] to be patient, which with extraordinary curteous usage, by little and little was wrought in her."

An Indian was then dispatched to let Powhatan know that the colonists had Pocahontas and that she would be "restored" if Powhatan would return the colonists whom he "detained in slaverie" together with "such armes and tooles as the Indians had gotten and stolne, and also a great quantity of corne."

Some time later, Powhatan returned seven colonists "with each of them a Musket unserviceable" plus "three peeces, one broad axe and a long whip-saw and one canow of corne" and passed word that when the colony "pleased to deliver his daughter," Powhatan would give, for the rest of the "pieces broken and stolne from him, 500 Bushells of Corne." But the colony, stating that Powhatan's daughter "was very well, and kindely intreated," replied that they "could not beleeve that the rest of our Arms were either lost, or stolne" from Powhatan, and "till he returned them all," the colony "would not by any meanes deliver his daughter."

Powhatan failed to reply, and in late March of 1614, Sir Thomas Dale, Marshall of Virginia and Deputy Governor, went with Argall's ship and some other vessels up into Powhatan's river (the Pamunkey), carrying Pocahontas as well as "an hundred and fifty men well appointed."

The Indians, "demaunding the cause of the our comming thither," were told that Dale proposed to "deliver Pocahontas" and to receive the colony's "Armes, men, & corn," . . . else Dale's men would fight and burn the Indians' houses, "take away their Canoas, breake downe their fishing Weares, and do them whatever damages" they could.

But the Indians asserted that they were "provided." And when the vessels entered the narrow part of the river, the Indians let fly their arrows, hitting one of Dale's men in the forehead, a wound which "might have hazarded his life without the present helpe of a skilfull Chirurgion."

Dale's men then went ashore, burned some forty houses, "made freeboote and pillage," and hurt or killed five or six Indians.

Finally, the flotilla sailing upriver "ancored neere unto the chiefest residencie Powhatan had, at a towne called Matchcot where were assembled . . . about 400 men, well appointed with their bowes and arrowes." And Dale's armed men, then "going up a high steepe hill," engaged the Indians in a consultation.

Pocahontas also "went ashore, but would not talke to any of" the Indians except to "them of the best sort, and to them onely," stating "that if her father had loved her, he would not value her lesse then olde swords, peeces, or axes: wherefore she would stil dwel with the English men, who loved her."[46]

In addition, two of Powhatan's sons, "being very desirous to see their sister . . . came unto us," and seeing Pocahontas and "her well fare" which they suspected to be worse . . . they much rejoyced", promising that "they would undoubtedly perswade their father to redeeme her."

Matzkot

In this one of the four pictures from EIN WARHAFFTIGER (1617) done by George Keller, Pocahontas is shown being seen by two of her brothers, and the small colonist, probably acting as an interpreter, probably is Thomas Savage. Courtesy Virginia State Library.

Meanwhile, "Maister John Rolfe and maister Sparkes," dispatched to "acquaint" Powhatan "with the businesse in hand," returned the next day, having been "kinley intreated," but having spoken only with Opecancanough.[47] However, some peace was made, and there may have been talk of marriage.

In 1612, Spain's ambassador at London reported that he was "credibly informed that there is a determination to marry [with Indians] some of the people that go over to Virginians; forty or fifty are already so married, and English women inter-mingle and are received kindly by the natives" and that "a zealous minister hath been wounded for reprehending it".[48]

Richard Pots and William Phettiplace, in a publication also dated 1612, stated

> Some propheticall spirit calculated he [Smith] had the Salvages in such subjection, hee would have made himselfe a king, by marrying Poca-hontas . . . It is true she was the very nomparell of his [Powhatan's] kingdome, and at most not past 13 or 14 yeares of age. Very oft shee came to our fort, with what shee could get for Captaine Smith . . . her especially he ever much respected . . . But her marriage could no way have intitled him to any right of the kingdome, nor was it ever suspected hee had ever such a thought . . . If he would he might have married her . . . For there was none that could have hindred his determination.[49]

However, in Virginia, Hamor noted that "a gentlemen of approved behaviour and honest carriage, maister John Rolfe" was "in love with Pocahontas and she with him."[50]

Rolfe, a tobacco plant experimenter, wrote a letter to Dale requesting marriage. In it Rolfe expressed his opinion that Pocahontas' "education hath bin rude, her manners barbarous, her generation accursed." He also discussed the interracial situation, alleging that his proposed marriage to Pocahontas was out of love, not out of lust. And finally he concluded that the marriage would be "for the good of this plantation, for the honour of our countrie, for the glory of God, for my owne salvacion, and for the converting to the true knowledge of God and Jesus Christ, an unbeleeving creature."[51]

For the marriage, Dale was "wel approving." Powhatan, engaged in fighting a constantly losing battle, suddenly consented. And Dale acted "milde" with Powhatan's Indians, stating that he "would not have departed their river without other conditions."[52]

Marriage of Pocahontas

A vignette from a french map done ca. 1739 by Jean Baptiste Nolin, Jr. Powhatan did not attend the wedding, the crowned figure probably is her uncle, the marriage should have been done in the church and the mountains in the background are perhaps a hundred miles out of place. The title translates:

SETTLEMENT
OF THE ENGLISH IN VIRGINIA

The English, wanting to take advantage of the riches all America was reputed to hold, started in 1585 to circulate in Virginia, but their first settlements were not very successful, and they were not able to establish a true colony before 1614, when they decided to marry Pocahontas, daughter of Powhatan, King of the Country, to an English gentleman named John Rolfe.

ETABLISSEMENT
DES ANGLOIS A LA VIRGINIE.

Les Anglois voulant profiter des Richesses que l'on s'imaginoit que toute l'Amerique devoit produire, commencerent en 1585. a naviguer en Virginie, mais leurs premiers etablissemens manquerent, et ils ne purent compter sur une colonie solide qu'en ...qu'ils s'aviserent de marier Pocahantas fille de Pontha...tan Roi du Pais a un Gentilhomme Anglois nommé Jean Rolfe.

As for the baptism, Reverend Alexander Whitaker noted that Dale "laboured along time to ground in" (make a Christian of) Pocahontas. Dale concluded that he "caused [Pocahontas] to be carefully instructed in Christian Religion, who after shee had made some good progresse therein, renounced publickly her countrey Idolatry, openly confessed her Christian faith, [and] was, as she desired, baptised." And fulfilling the Old World determination that the only good given name was one found in the Bible, Dale and perhaps other authorities gave Pocahontas the name Rebecca.

Prior to the marriage, Powhatan sent Pocahontas' "olde uncle . . . named Opachisco, to give her as his deputy in the Church, and two of his [Powhatan's] sonnes to see the marriage solemnized."[53]

As for the marriage which took place on April 5, Dale noted it as "an other knot to binde this peace the stronger." And later, Dale reported that Pocahontas "lives civilly and lovingly with" Rolfe.[54]

In May, Hamor visited Powhatan, accompanied by two Indian guides and by Thomas Savage, who had lived three years with Powhatan and acted as interpreter.

Following the usual gift-giving and small talk, Powhatan inquired about Pocahontas' "welfare, her mariage, his unknowne sonne, and how they liked, lived and loved together." Hamor replied that Pocahontas was "so well content that she would not change her life to return and live with" Powhatan.

"Whereat," Powhatan "laughed heartily, and said he was very glad of it."

But the main purpose of Hamor's visit was to see if Powhatan would give "the exquisite perfection" of his "yongest daughter, being famous through all your territories," to Dale, "partly for the desire which he [Dale] himselfe hath, and partly for the desire her sister hath to see her."

This youngest daughter, "not full twelve years old," was to be Dale's "neerest companion, wife and bedfellow," but Powhatan's answer was that "within these few daies" she is " to be wife to a great Werowance for two bushels of Roanoke," and "is already gone with him."

Powhatan loved Pocahontas but he loved also his youngest daughter "as deere as his owne life, and though he had many Children, he delighted in none so much as in her, whom if he should not often beholde, he could not possibly live, which she living with us he knew he could not, having with himselfe resolved upon no termes whatsoever to put himselfe into our hands, or come amongst us."

Powhatan held "it not a brotherly part" of Dale "to desire to bereave me of two of my children at once," recalling that Dale "hath a pledge" of daughter Pocahontas, and as long as she lives, she "shall be sufficient." But when "she dieth he shall have another childe of mine."

Powhatan closed by saying "there have bin too many of his [Dale's] men and my [men] killed, which by my occasion ther shall never bee more . . . for I am now olde, and would gladly end my daies in peace, so as if the English offer me injury, my country is large enough, I will remove my selfe farther from you," Powhatan hopes being that all gifts and promises would "give him [Dale] good satisfaction, if it doe not I will goe three daies journy farther from him, and never see English men more."

When Hamor and Savage "were ready to depart," Powhatan "gave each of them an excellent Bucks skin, very well dressed, and white as snow, and sent his sonne and daughter each of them one."[55]

As for Dale, he already had a wife in England.

In June 1614, Hamor left for England. Rolfe succeeded him as the Colony's secretary and recorder. In late 1614 or early in 1615, Pocahontas gave birth to a child named Thomas, probably for Dale. And in the spring of 1616, Dale took to England not only Pocahontas, her child, and her husband, John Rolfe, but also her sister Matchama, her sister's husband and Powhatan's priest-counsellor Tomocomo,[56] and several young Powhatan Indian men and women.

Soon after June 3, 1616, the day the ship landed at Plymouth, Tomocomo got "a long sticke" and kept "by notches" a record of all the English persons he could see. But of that task, Tomocomo became "quickly weary."

Tomocomo was also instructed by Powhatan "to seeke" Smith in order to determine if Smith was still alive. Powhatan and his people had "alwaies" been told by the colonists that Smith was dead but Powhatan, knowing that the colonists "will lie much," wanted to ascertain the truth.

And Pocahontas "knew no other," i.e., did not know Smith was alive, "till I came to Plimouth."[57]

Smith, learning of Pocahontas Plymouth landing, wrote a "little book" to King James' Danish consort, Queen Anne, detailing Pocahontas' kindnesses, and stating that for:

> two or three yeeres, she next under God, was still the instrument to preserve this Colonie from death, famine and utter confusion . . .

> . . . after she . . . was taken prisoner . . . the Colonie by that meanes was relieued, peace concluded; and at lest rejecting her barbarous condition, [Pocahontas] was maried to an English Gentleman, with whom at this present she is in England; the first Christian ever of that Nation, the first Virginian ever spake English, or had a childe in mariage by an English-man . . .[58]

> . . . this might bee presented you from a more worthy pen, it cannot from a more honest heart . . .

> her husbands estate not being able to make her fit to attend your Maiestie . . .

> . . . if she should not be well received . . . her present love to us and Christianitie, might turne to such scorne and furie, as to divert all this good to the worst of evill . . . .[59]

In London, Pocahontas and her group of Indians were not completely novel. As early as 1497, some Indians of North America had been displayed in London. Later on, in 1603, two Indians were produced in London. In 1605, George Weymouth brought from Maine to London five Abnaki Indians. On April 10, 1608, Newport brought Namontack to England where they stayed for six months. And in 1609, Smith sent Namontack back to England accompanying him with another Powhatan Indian named Matchumps.[60]

As for female Indians, one of the five Abnakis, "Mrs. Panobscot" dressed as an Elizabethan and had a full-length portrait painted.[61]

But Pocahontas was not just an Indian or a Powhatan Indian, she was a princess, and "by the diligent care of Master John Rolfe . . . and his friends," she was "taught to speake such English as might well bee understood," was "well instructed in Christianitie", and became "very formall and civill after our English manner."[62]

However, there was "the poore companie."

"Out of theyre povertie are faine to allow her fowre pound a weeke for her maintenance."[63] And in a move that may have been impecunious if not racist, Pocahontas was lodged at the heavily patronized tavern known since long prior to her visit as the Belle Sauvage.

But a princess in a tavern!

In Ben Johnson's comedy, *The Staple of News*, first performed in 1625, a young man considers taking a lady (a "princess") to eat at lawyer Picklock's lodging, but the young man's father (Pennyboy Canter) objects:

Pennyboy Canter: Let your meat rather follow you to a tavern.

Picklock: A tavern's as unfit too for a princess.

Pennyboy Canter: No I have known a princess, and a great one, Come forth of a tavern.

Picklock: Not go in, sir, though.

Pennyboy Canter: She must go in, if she came forth: the blessed Pokahontas, as the historian calls her, And great king's daughter of Virginia, Hath been in womb of tavern . . .[64]

Tavern or not, Pocahontas was kindly treated by "divers other persons of good qualities both publikely at the maskes and otherwise."[65] John Chamberlain, one of the Company's stockholders, described Pocahontas as "the most remarquable person."[66] The Lord Bishop of London entertained Pocahontas "with festivall state and pompe, beyond . . . his great hospitalitie afforded other Ladies."[67] And as a possible result of Smith's "little book," "it pleased both the King and Queenes Majestie honourably to esteeme" Pocahontas who was then "accompanied with that honourable Lady [Ceclie] the Lady De La Warre, and that honourable Lord her husband."

Pocahontas and Tomocomo, who dressed and acted as Powhatan's counsellor, were "with the King and graciously used." They were "well placed at the masque." And according to Smith, the several entertainments were done to Pocahontas' "great satisfaction and content."[68]

But soon illness struck. In 1616, three Indians "brought from Virginia by Dale" died at the house of Sir Thomas Smythe, in Philpot Lane, Langhorne Ward, and were buried at St. Dinos Church.[69] Possibly after the 1616 holiday season, Pocahontas and at least some of her Indians were moved on up the Thames into the village of Brentford. And there Pocahontas was visited by John Smith.

Smith, since recovering from his wounding, had been exploring, fishing, and traveling mainly for the Plymouth-headquartered group that had the "rights" to settle what Smith labelled New England. And during Pocahontas' early English months, Smith was "preparing to set saile for New England," and "could not stay to doe" for her "that service I desired, and she well deserved." But late in 1616 or early in 1617, Smith, hearing that Pocahontas was at Brentford, went "with divers of my friends," and paid her a visit.

"Pocahontas, after a modest salutation, without any word she turned about, obscured her face, as not seeming well contented; and in that humhor, her husband, with divers others" (including Smith) "left her two or three hours."

Smith meanwhile "repenting my selfe to have writ she could speake English."

"But not long after, she began to talke, and remembered mee [Smith] well what countesies shee had done," stating "You did promise Powhatan what was yours should bee his, and he the like to you; you called him father being in his land a stranger, and by the same reason so I must doe you."

Smith wrote, "I durst not allow that title" to be used, because she "was a Kings daughter."

Pocahontas continued "with a well set countenance," and said, "Were you not afraid to come into my fathers Countrie, and caused feare in him and all his people (but mee), and feare you here I should call you father; I tell you then I will, and you shall call mee childe, and so I will bee for ever and ever your Countrieman."

Powhatan had also instructed Tomocomo to "find" Smith and if successful, he was to have Smith show him the English God, King, Queen, and Prince. And when, by chance, Tomocomo and Smith met in London, Smith explained about "God the best I could."

Tomocomo then stated that "by circumstances he was satisfied he had seen the King," but Tomocomo "replyed very sadly, you gave Powhatan a white Dog, which Powhatan fed as himselfe: but your King gave me nothing, and I am better than your white Dog."

During "the small time [Smith] staid in London, divers Courtiers and others, [Smith's] acquaintances, hath gone with" Smith to see Pocahontas and "generally concluded, they did thinke God had a great hand in her conversion, and they have seene many English Ladies worse favoured, proportioned and behavioured." [70]

This engraving, done in 1616 and "designed or executed" by Simon van de Passe, differs slightly from the often-duplicated colored oil Booten Hall painting which probably was a copy of the engraving or of a drawing. Other Pocahontas drawings or engravings may well have been done, and one cannot say for sure that the "fine picture" which John Chamberlain sent on February 22, 1617 was a copy of the van de Passe engraving.

Pocahontas in England, in the winter of 1616-17, might be more properly dressed in a feather mantle than if she was wearing English court clothes plus a top hat. Mc-Cary, at page 17, states: "Mantles of turkey feathers were occasionally worn by the chiefs and by men and women of distinction". One guess is that this portrait was done in Holland in the late 1600's and another guess is that it was used as a tavern sign.

Sometime during 1616, Simon van de Passe made an engraving of Pocahontas—he recorded her age as twenty-one. And on February 22, 1617, Chamberlain sent "a fine picture of a no fair Lady" noting that "with her tricking up and high style and titles you might think her and her worshipful husband to be somebody."[71]

At some point, it is probable that Pocahontas travelled the one hundred miles to Norfolk County, to the village of Heacham, and to Heacham Hall, the Rolfe family abode.[72]

At any event, Pocahontas, her child "which she loved most deerely,"[73] her husband, and some of their attendants were scheduled to return to Virginia aboard Argall's *George*, the flagship of a fleet of three vessels.

In a letter dated January 18, 1617, Chamberlain wrote that Pocahontas was "upon her return though sore against her will."[74]

Then, in a letter dated March 26, 1617, Chamberlain reported, "The Virginian woman whose picture I sent you, died last week at Gravesend, as she was returning homeward . . . ."[75]

Gravesend, gloomily named, is located in Kent on the Thames River some twenty-five miles downstream from London. And the March 21, 1617 St. George's Parish Register reads, "Rebecca Wrothe wyff of Thomas Wroth gent a Virginia lady borne, here was buried in ye chauncell."[76]

The names "Wrothe" and "Thomas Wroth" are perhaps best described as clerical errors.

AFTERWORD

Because of the continued illness of Thomas Rolfe ("the lyving ashes of his deceased Mother") and of his attendants, John Rolfe was "much ymportuned" to leave Thomas at Gravesend. However, all hands headed off on the one hundred and seventy-odd mile trip to Plymouth, and although the *George* encountered "smoothe water," John Rolfe soon "found such feare and hazard of his [Thomas'] health (being not fully recovered of his sickness) and lack of attendance (for they who looked to him hadd need of nurses themselves . . .) that by the advise of Captaine Argall, and divers who also foresaw the danger and knew the inconvenyence thereof p'swaded" him to leave Thomas in Plymouth, and with Sir Lewis Stukeley, Vice Admiral of Devon.

John Rolfe in a later letter lamented his wife's death, and wrote that the presence of his son Thomas was "much desired when he is of better strength to endure so hard a passage."[77]

Soon Thomas was living in London under the care of his merchant uncle Henry.

All the while, and up to 1620, the Company was taking care of one of Pocahontas' Indian maids "who sometimes dwelt a servant with a mercer in Cheapside, (and) is now very weake of a consumption." Two other "Virginia maydes havinge bynne a longe time verie chargeable to ye Company" were "sent to the Summer Illands whyther they were willinge to goe with our servants . . . towards their preferm't in marriage with such as shall accept of them."[78] And Smith later reported that one was married "with a husband fit for her, attended with more then one hundred guests, and all the dainties for their dinner could be provided."[79]

In London, in September of 1632, Thomas Rolfe, who may or may not have been Pocahontas' son, married Elizabeth Washington. In about 1635, Pocahontas' son Thomas returned to Virginia, and in 1655 he had a daughter Jane, who in 1675 married Colonel Robert Bolling and had numerous descendants.[80]

By that date, the once-powerful Virginia Indians had been almost completely destroyed by imported diseases, colonists' wars, and moral disintegration.

PATAWOMECKE
TRIBE △

POTOMAC RIVER

RAPPAHANNOCK
TRIBE
△

MATTAPONI RIVER

RAPPAHANNOCK RIVER

PAMUNKEY RIVER

CHICKAHOMINY RIVER

CHESAPEAKE BAY

WEROWO-
COMOCO ○
R
I
V
E
R

PASPAHEGH
TRIBE
△

APPOMATTUCK
TRIBE △

JAMES

JAMES-
TOWN

RIVER

ATLANTIC OCEAN

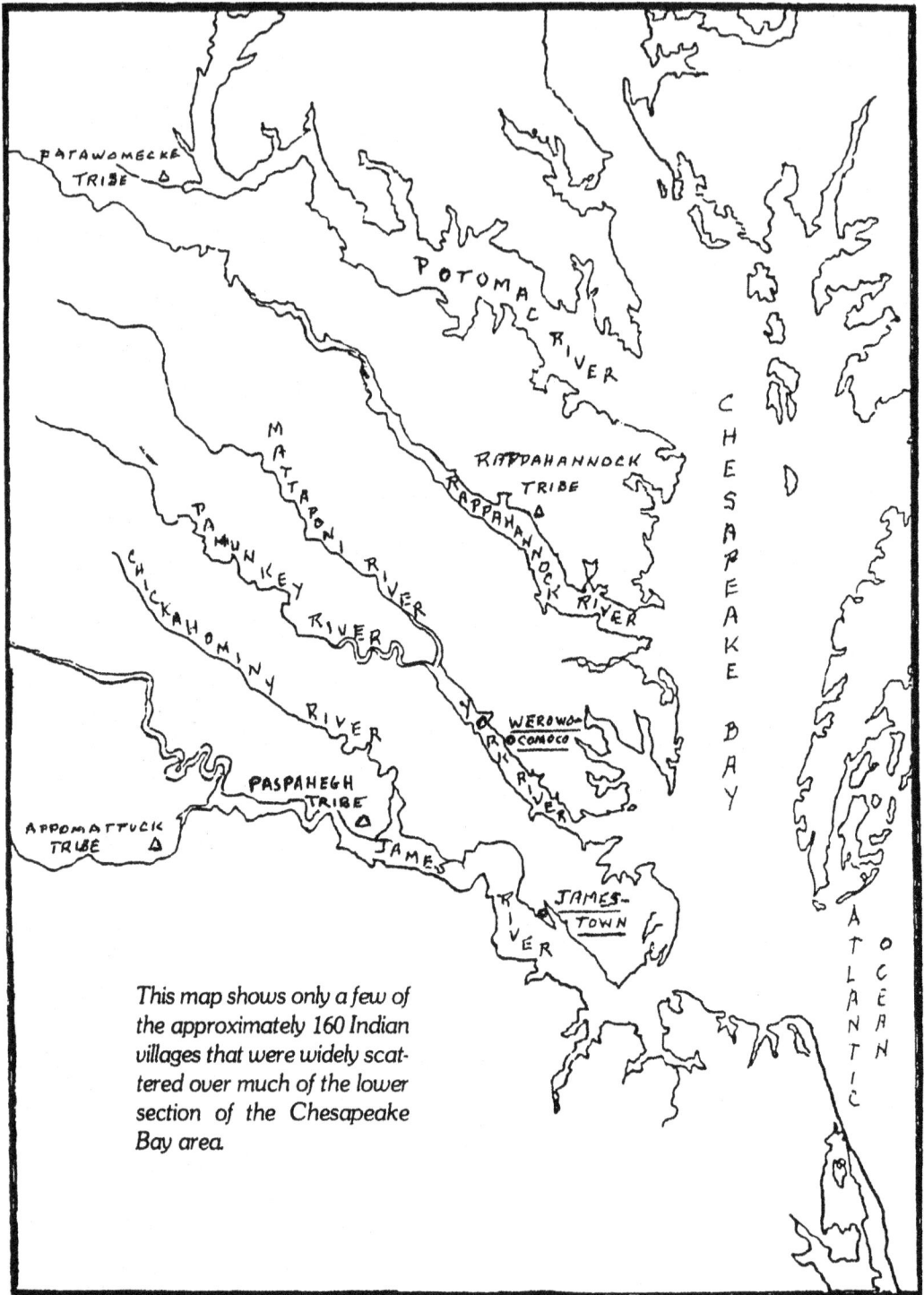

This map shows only a few of the approximately 160 Indian villages that were widely scattered over much of the lower section of the Chesapeake Bay area.

SHORT-TITLE INDEX

BARBOUR—Barbour, Philip L. POCAHONTAS AND HER WORLD. 1970.

CHAMBERLAIN—Chamberlain, John. THE LETTERS OF JOHN CHAMBERLAIN. Ed. by Norman Egbert McClure. 2 vols. 1939.

HAMOR—Hamor, Ralph. A TRUE DISCOURSE OF THE PRESENT STATE OF VIRGINIA. 1957. Reprint of 1615 edition.

McCARY—McCary, Ben C. INDIANS IN SEVENTEENTH-CENTURY VIRGINIA. 1957.

MOSSIKER—Mossiker, Frances. POCAHONTAS: THE LIFE AND THE LEGEND. 1976.

NEILL—Neill, Edward D. HISTORY OF THE VIRGINIA COMPANY OF LONDON, WITH LETTERS TO AND FROM THE FIRST COLONY NEVER BEFORE PRINTED. 1869.

PERCY—Percy, George. A TREWE RELACYON OF THE PROCEDEINGES AND OCURRENTES OF MOMENTE WHICH HAVE HAPNED IN VIRGINIA FROM . . . 1609 UNTIL . . . 1612. TYLER'S QUARTERLY MAGAZINE (1922) III: 259-282.

QUINN—Quinn, David Beers. SET FAIRE FOR ROANOKE: VOYAGES AND COLONIES 1584-1606. 1985.

SMITH (ARBER ed.)—Smith,. John. TRAVELS AND WORKS OF CAPTAIN JOHN SMITH. Ed. by Edward Arber and A.G. Bradley. 2 vols. 1910.

SMITH (BARBOUR ed.)—Smith, John. THE COMPLETE WORKS OF CAPTAIN JOHN SMITH (1580-1631). Ed. by Philip L. Barbour. 3 vols. 1986.

STRACHEY—Strachey, William. THE HISTORIE OF TRAVELL INTO VIRGINIA BRITANIA (1612) Ed. by Louis B. Wright and Virginia Freund. 1953.

WOODWARD—Woodward, Grace Steele. POCAHONTAS. 1968.

An extensive Pocahontas bibliography is to be found in *BARBOUR, MOSSIKER* and *WOODWARD,* and an extensive Captain John Smith bibliography is included in Volume III of *SMITH (BARBOUR ed.).*

NOTES

1. *STRACHEY* 63, 70-2 and 113. *SMITH* (*ARBER* ed.) lxix and lxx. *McCARY* 26-35. Pocahontas' exact age is not known.
2. *MOSSIKER* 41. Statements in *STRACHEY* or perhaps language difficulties indicate some misunderstanding as regards the identity of Powhatan's daughter. On page 114, according to Strachey, Powhatan "called a young daughter of his, whome he loved well Pochahuntas, which may signifie Little-wanton, howbeit she was rightly called Amonute". On page 62, Strachey recites the marriage of "Pocahunta" to Koucoum. And on page 72, Strachey, using the name "Pochohuntas", tells of the cartwheel incident. On that page the editors of *STRACHEY*, Louis B. Wright and Virginia Freund, state that "others beside the Indian girl who married John Rolfe . . . seem to have borne the name", and they doubt that the girl who married Koucoum was the same as Matoaka who married John Rolfe. Were Matoaka and Amonute the same person? Was the Indian girl who married John Rolfe and the cartwheel girl the same person?
3. *MOSSIKER* 28. *WOODWARD* 9. Powhatan's tribes were "Northeast Woodlands", and their total number about equalled the number of Iroquoian and Siouan Indians who inhabited the remaining four-fifths of what is now the Commonwealth of Virginia.
4. *STRACHEY* 62-3. Writing in 1612, Strachey states that Powhatan had then living twenty sons and twelve daughters. Powhatan's name was Wahunsonacock but he was commonly referred to by the name of his tribe, i.e., the Powhatan tribe.
5. *SMITH* (*ARBER* ed.) lxi.
6. Lewis, Clifford M.; and Loomis, Albert J. *THE SPANISH JESUIT MISSION IN VIRGINIA 1570-1572.* 1953.
7. *SMITH* (*BARBOUR* ed.) I:51.
8. *QUINN* 356. These captives were taken to London, probably in a ship commanded by Samuel Mace.
9. *SMITH* (*BARBOUR* ed.) I:55.
10. *SMITH* (*ARBER* ed.) lxviii.
11. *NEILL* 11.
12. *SMITH* (*ARBER* ed.) lxxv and lxxvi.
13. *STRACHEY* 72.
14. *STRACHEY* 72.
15. *NEILL* 12.
16. *SMITH* (*ARBER* ed.) lxxii.
17. *SMITH* (*BARBOUR* ed.) I:47 and II:146-7 and 150-1.
18. *SMITH* (*BARBOUR* ed.) II: 258-60.
19. *SMITH* (*BARBOUR* ed.) I:173.
20. *SMITH* (*BARBOUR* ed.) I:153.
21. *SMITH* (*ARBER* ed.) xlix and 1.
22. *SMITH* (*BARBOUR* ed.) II:151 and II:258-60. The saving of Smith by Pocahontas is not reported in *A TRUE RELATION OF SUCH OCCURRENCES AND ACCIDENTS OF NOATE AS HATH HAPNED IN VIRGINIA* (1608) ("published without Smith's knowledge, permission, or supervisions" and "ruthlessly edited and hastily and badly printed"). But in *NEW ENGLAND'S TRIALS* (1622) Smith writes that the Indians "slue three of my men and . . . tooke me prisoner; yet God made Pocahontas . . . the meanes to deliver me." And in Smith's 1624 book, the saving is detailed. *BARBOUR* 24 states that the saving was the first meeting of Pocahontas and Smith but *WOODWARD* 71 states that Pocahontas acted "doubtless out of gratitude for his kindness to her", an indication that Pocahontas and Smith had met before, and this is a possible indication that the cartwheel exhibition preceeded the saving. *BARBOUR* 260: "The [saving] story comes from Smith's *GENERALL HISTORIE*, which contains so much information about Pocahontas not to be found in his previous works that its truthfulness has sometimes been questioned. I am inclined to believe that the *GENERALL HISTORIE* is basically sound, but contains no small amount of elaboration. A well-told story is not fundamentally untrue merely because it has been elaborated." Smith's *A MAP OF VIRGINIA* (1612) includes an Indian language phrase which translates: Bid Pokahontas bring hither two little Baskets, and I will give her white beads to make her a chaine. *SMITH* (*BARBOUR* ed.) I:139.
23. *SMITH* (*BARBOUR* ed.) II:151. Capahowosick is shown on Smith's map as being some miles east of Werowcomoco. *SMITH* (*ARBER* ed.) 384.
24. *SMITH* (*BARBOUR* ed.) II:258-60. When a reference is made to Pocahontas' "brother" or "sister," it probably means her half-brother or half-sister. *McCARY* 49-50 tells us that "a werowance never had but one child by the same wife," and that "when the child reaches a certain age, it was taken from the mother and placed in charge of the werowance . . . the mother was free to marry again". Nothing is known about Pocahontas' mother.
25. *SMITH* (*BARBOUR* ed.) II: 259.

26. Purchas, Samuel. *PURCHAS HIS PILGRIMAGE* (1614 ed.) 767.
27. *SMITH (ARBER* ed.) 1xxxvi.
28. *SMITH (BARBOUR* ed.) II:152.
29. *SMITH (BARBOUR* ed.) II:259.
30. *SMITH (BARBOUR* ed.) II:151.
31. *SMITH (BARBOUR* ed.) II:156.
32. *SMITH (BARBOUR* ed.) I:93.
33. *SMITH (BARBOUR* ed.) I:160.
34. *SMITH (BARBOUR* ed.) I:95.
35. *SMITH (BARBOUR* ed.) I:182-3.
36. *SMITH (BARBOUR* ed.) II:184.
37. *SMITH (BARBOUR* ed.) II:198-9.
38. *SMITH (BARBOUR* ed.) II:203.
39. *SMITH (BARBOUR* ed.) II:223-4. *PERCY* 264.
40. *SMITH (ARBER* ed.) ciii.
41. *SMITH (BARBOUR* ed.) II:259. *STRACHEY* 62.
42. *PERCY* 267.
43. *SMITH (BARBOUR* ed.) II:232.
44. Pocahontas' abduction and the Matchcot meeting are set forth in *HAMOR* 4-8 and *NEILL* 86-7.
45. *HAMOR* 9. "MatchCot" was "at the head almost of the Pamaunkie River." *HAMOR* 38.
46. *HAMOR* 53-4.
47. *HAMOR* 10.
48. *NEILL* 85.
49. *SMITH (BARBOUR* ed.) I:274.
50. *HAMOR* 10.
51. This letter is reproduced in full in *HAMOR* 61-68 and in *BARBOUR* 247-252. Edward Duffield Neill described it as "a labored treatise" having "the musty smell of the dusty study of a London divine, rather than the fragrance of a letter written by a man in love."
52. *HAMOR* 11.
53. *HAMOR* 11.
54. *HAMOR* 55-6 and 59-60. Recent investigations cast doubts upon the statement that the Rolfes lived upriver on the property known as Varina.
55. *HAMOR* 40-2 and 46.
56. Tomocomo's name was Uttamatomakkin.
57. *SMITH* II:261.
58. Some portion of these three statements made by Smith might possibly be incorrect.
59. *SMITH (BARBOUR* ed.) II:259-60.
60. Some "differences fell betweene" Namontack and Matchumps, and in 1610, in the Bermuda Islands, Matchumps slew Namontack and having "made a hole to bury him, because it [the hole] was too short, he cut off [Namontack's] legs and laid them by him, which murder he concealed till he was in Virginia." *SMITH (BARBOUR* ed.) II:350.
61. *MOSSIKER* 222. *WOODWARD* 172.
62. *SMITH (BARBOUR* ed.) II:258.
63. *CHAMBERLAIN* II:57.
64. *BARBOUR* 160.
65. *SMITH (BARBOUR* ed.) II:262.
66. *MOSSIKER* 218.
67. Purchas, Samuel. *HAKLUYTUS POSTHUMUS, OR PURCHAS HIS PILGRIMES.* 1653. IV:1774.
68. *SMITH (BARBOUR* ed.) II:261-2.
69. *MOSSIKER* 236.
70. *SMITH (BARBOUR* ed.) II:260-1.
71. *CHAMBERLAIN* II:57. The word "fair" may indicate either that Pocahontas skin was tawny or that Chamberlain did not consider her to be pretty or that she was ill at the time the artist depicted her.
72. *MOSSIKER* 267-9. *BARBOUR* 161.
73. *SMITH (BARBOUR* ed.) II:258.
74. *NEILL* 97. "Sore against her will" may indicate that Pocahontas, her child and their Indian attendants were ill, and that she feared an ocean voyage.
75. *CHAMBERLAIN* II:66-7. The cause of Pocahontas' death is not known but a good supposition is that her throat and lungs were irritated by London's noxious fumes, and that her death resulted from an acute respiratory or pulmonary attack. *MOSSIKER* 255, 275 and 277. *WOODWARD* 184.
76. *NEILL* 98. Compare *MOSSIKER* 281.
77. *VIRGINIA MAGAZINE OF HISTORY AND BIOGRAPHY* (1903) X:137.
78. *NEILL* 102-4.
79. *SMITH (BARBOUR* ed.) I:386.
80. Brief material on Thomas Rolfe and much material on his descendants is contained in the book *POCAHONTAS' DESCENDANTS* (1985) by Stuart E. Brown, Jr., Lorraine F. Myers and Eileen M. Chappel, and in its *SUPPLEMENT* (1987) by the same writers.

www.ingramcontent.com/pod-product-compliance
Lightning Source LLC
Chambersburg PA
CBHW050357100426
42739CB00015BB/3430